ANIMALS
THAT LIVE ON THE
FARM

Cows

JoAnn Early Macken

**Reading consultant: Susan Nations, M.Ed.,
author/literacy coach/consultant**

WEEKLY WR READER®
EARLY LEARNING LIBRARY

Please visit our web site at: www.earlyliteracy.cc
For a free color catalog describing Weekly Reader® Early Learning Library's list
of high-quality books, call 1-877-445-5824 (USA) or 1-800-387-3178 (Canada).
Weekly Reader® Early Learning Library's fax: (414) 336-0164.

Library of Congress Cataloging-in-Publication Data

Macken, JoAnn Early, 1953–
   Cows / JoAnn Early Macken.
     p. cm. — (Animals that live on the farm)
   Includes bibliographical references and index.
   ISBN 0-8368-4272-3 (lib. bdg.)
   ISBN 0-8368-4279-0 (softcover)
   1. Cattle—Juvenile literature. 2. Cows—Juvenile literature. I. Title. II. Series.
SF197.5.M325   2004
636.2—dc22   2004043763

This edition first published in 2005 by
Weekly Reader® Early Learning Library
330 West Olive Street, Suite 100
Milwaukee, WI 53212 USA

Copyright © 2005 by Weekly Reader® Early Learning Library

Picture research: Diane Laska-Swanke
Art direction: Tammy West
Cover design and page layout: Kami Koenig

Photo credits: Cover, pp. 7, 11, 13, 15, 17, 19 Gregg Andersen;
pp. 5, 9 © Alan & Sandy Carey; p. 21 © James P. Rowan

Printed in the United States of America

1 2 3 4 5 6 7 8 9 08 07 06 05 04

Note to Educators and Parents

Reading is such an exciting adventure for young children! They are beginning to integrate their oral language skills with written language. To encourage children along the path to early literacy, books must be colorful, engaging, and interesting; they should invite the young reader to explore both the print and the pictures.

Animals That Live on the Farm is a new series designed to help children read about the behavior and life cycles of farm animals. Each book describes a different type of animal and explains why and how it is raised.

Each book is specially designed to support the young reader in the reading process. The familiar topics are appealing to young children and invite them to read — and re-read — again and again. The full-color photographs and enhanced text further support the student during the reading process.

In addition to serving as wonderful picture books in schools, libraries, homes, and other places where children learn to love reading, these books are specifically intended to be read within an instructional guided reading group. This small group setting allows beginning readers to work with a fluent adult model as they make meaning from the text. After children develop fluency with the text and content, the book can be read independently. Children and adults alike will find these books supportive, engaging, and fun!

— Susan Nations, M.Ed., author, literacy coach, and consultant in literacy development

Cows are female cattle. Bulls are male cattle. A baby cow is called a **calf**.

A calf can stand
soon after it is born.
It drinks milk from
its mother.

In warm weather, cows stay outside. They graze on grass. They swish their tails to flick away flies.

Cows lie down
to rest. They
face away
from the wind.

In cold weather, cows stay in a barn. Most farmers feed cows hay, corn, and oats.

After a cow eats, it burps up its food. Then it chews the food again. The food it chews is called its **cud**.

Cows spend most of the day eating or chewing. They drink lots of water every day.

Farmers keep cows for meat and milk. Farmers milk the cows twice a day.

Some people use cattle to pull heavy loads. Have you ever seen cows on a farm?

Glossary

cattle — animals such as oxen or cows that chew their cud and are kept on a farm or a ranch

graze — to eat grass

hay — grass that is cut and dried for food

For More Information

Books

Cow. Malachy Doyle (Margaret K. McElderry)

Cow. Jules Older (Charlesbridge)

Kiss the Cow. Phyllis Root (Candlewick)

Milk. Where Does Our Food Come From? (series). Gretchen Will Mayo (Weekly Reader Early Learning Library)

Web Sites

Got Milk?
www.got-milk.com/
Cow and milk facts, games, and recipes

Index

About the Author

JoAnn Early Macken is the author of two rhyming picture books, *Sing-Along Song* and *Cats on Judy*, and four other series of nonfiction books for beginning readers. Her poems have appeared in several children's magazines. A graduate of the M.F.A. in Writing for Children and Young Adults program at Vermont College, she lives in Wisconsin with her husband and their two sons. Visit her Web site at www.joannmacken.com.